original edition 194

NAVAJO LIFE

Pre-Primer

By

HILDEGARD THOMPSON

BUREAU OF INDIAN AFFAIRS

Andrew Tsihnajinnie working on a painting in 1934

Created by Native Child Dinétah, Flagstaff, AZ 86003

www.nativechild.com   info@nativechild.com

by Hildegard Thompson

illustrated by Andrew Tsihnajinnie

Design, Layout and Cover Art by Bernhard Michaelis

Colorization by Dalasie Michaelis

Originally published by the Education Division – US Office of Indian Affairs 1946.
Title: Navajo Life Series Pre–Primer

ISBN 978-1497581456

Kee is a Navajo boy.

Kii Naabeehó 'ashkii át'é.

Bah is a Navajo girl.

Baa' Naabeehó 'at'ééd 'át'é.

This is Bah's mother.
She is Kee's mother, too.

Díí Baa' bimá 'át'é.
Kii dó' bimá 'át'é.

This is Kee's father.
He is Bah's father, too.

Díí Kii bizhé'é 'át'é.
Baa' dó' bizhé'é 'át'é.

Mother and father live in a hogan.
It is Kee and Bah's hogan.

Bimá dóó bizhé'é hooghan yii' bighan.
'Éí Kii dóó Baa' bighan.

Mother and father have many sheep.

Bimá dóó bizhé'é bidibé t'óó 'ahayóí.

Mother and father have goats.
The goats are fat.

Bimá dóó bizhé'é bitł'ízí dó' hóló.
Tł'ízí 'éí daneesk'ah.

Bah and Kee herd the goats and sheep.

Baa' dóó Kii tł'ízí dóó dibé neiniłkaad.

**Bah and Kee play
when they herd the sheep.**

**Baa' dóó Kii dibé neiniłkaadgo
naanée łeh.**

Kee has a dog.
The dog and Kee herd the sheep.

Kii bilééchąą'í hólǫ́.
Kii bilééchąą'í yił dibé neiniłkaad łeh.

Father has two horses.
They are fat horses.

Bizhé'é łį́į́' naaki bee hólǫ́.
Łį́į́' 'éi neesk'ah.

Father has a wagon.
It is pretty.

Bizh'é'é bitsinaabąąs hólǫ́.
'Éí nizhóní.

This is the trader.
He lives at the trading post.

Díí naalyéhé yá sidáhí 'át'é.
Naalyéhé bá hooghandi bighan.

Father, mother, Kee and Bah go to the trading post. They go in the wagon.

Kii dóó Baa' dóó bizhé'é dóó bimá naalyéhé bá hooghangóó 'ałnánákah. Tsinaabáás yee 'ałnánákah.

Father buys things from the trader.
The trader buys things from father.

Bizhé'é t'áadoo le'é naalyéhé yá sidáhí
yaa nináyiiłnih. Naalyéhé yá sidáhí dó'
kii bizhé'é t'áadoo le'é yaa nináyiiłnih.

Andrew Tsihnajinnie (1916–2000)

Born in Rough Rock in 1916, Arizona, Andrew Van Tsinahjinnie had been drawing since he was a child. As a small boy he drew on the backs of canned food labels and wrapping paper his mother bought at the trading post. He went to boarding school at Fort Apache for elementary education and then to Santa Fe Indian School. According to his daughter Hulleah, he escaped from Fort Apache school just to be picked up again by police at his home. Only 8 years old, he was put into prison in Chinle, shackled and handcuffed and was taken back to the school in present day Whiteriver, Arizona on the White Mountain Apache Reservation, 250 miles away from his home.

He studied with Dorothy Dunn at the Studio in Santa Fe where he was one of the Navajo students. Tsihnajinnie exhibeted skill and an innnate facility with drawing figures. He graduated in 1936. Even before he went into the army in 1941, Tsinahjinnie had done murals in Indian Hospitals. After the service he studied at the Oakland College of Arts and Crafts in California.

Since 1977 he suffered with a serious illness and had not been able to do much painting or teaching, but he kept his love of the traditional Navajo ways. Tsinahjinnie grew up herding sheep and riding horses and his love for that life was what he portrayed in his paintings. He was married to Minnie McGirt and they had seven children.

Rewarded the Arizona Living Treasure title, the artist has work included in the permanent collections of the Denver Art Museum; the Thomas Gilcrease Institute of American History and Art in Tulsa, Oklahoma; the Heard Museum in Phoenix, Arizona; the Museum of Northern Arizona in Flagstaff, Arizona; the Philbrook Museum of Art in Tulsa; the Millicent Rogers Foundation Museum in Taos, New Mexico; the Smithsonian Institution in Washington, DC and the Wheelwright Museum of the American Indian Art in Santa Fe—just to name a few.

Tsihnajinnie worked for many years at the Rough Rock demonstration school in Rough Rock, Arizona, the first self regulated bilingual Native American school in the United States.

VOCABULARY

A

'ałnánákah, they go back and forth (repeatedly).

'ashkii, boy.

'át'é, he is; she is; it is; they are.

'at'ééd, girl.

B

Baa', Bah (feminine name).

bidibé, his sheep; her sheep; their sheep.

bighan, his home; her home; their home.

bilééchąą'í, his dog; her dog; their dog.

bilį́į́', his horse; her horse; their horse (pet or livestock).

bimá, his mother; her mother. their mother.

bitł'ízí, his goat; her goat; their goat.

bitsinaabąąs, his wagon; her wagon; their wagon.

bizhé'é, his father; her father; their father.

D

daneesk'ah, they are fat.

dibé, sheep.

díí, this; these.

dó', too; also.

dóó, and.

E

'éí, that; those.

H

hólǫ́, there is; there are.

hooghan, home; hogan.

K

Kii, Kee (masculine name).

Ł

łeh, usually; customarily.

N

Naabeehó, Navajo.

naaki, two.

naalyéhé yá sidáhí, trader.

naalyéhé bá hooghandi, at the trading post.

naalyéhé bá hooghangóó, to the trading post.

naané, he plays; she plays; they play.

neesk'ah, he is fat; she is fat; they are fat.

neiniłkaad, he herds them; she herds them; they herd them.

neiniłkaadgo, when he (she or they) herd(s) them.

nináyiiłnih, he trades it; she trades it; they trade it (buy or sell it). yaa nináyiiłnih, he (she or they) buy(s) it from him (them).

nizhóní, he is pretty; she is pretty; they are pretty (clean or nice).

T

t'áadoo le'é, things; something.

tł'ízí, goat; goats.

t'óó 'ahayói, many; much.

Y

yaa, he to him; she to her; they to them.

yee, (he) by means of it; with it.

yii', (he) inside of it; in it.

yił, he with him; she with her; they with them (in company with).

The Navaho Alphabet

The following information with regard to the Navaho alphabet and its use should prove helpful to one familiar with the English language.

Vowels

The vowels have continental values. They are as follows, the first example being a Navaho word, the second the closest approximation to the sound in an English word:

a	gad	(juniper)	father
e	ké	(shoe)	met
i	sis	(belt) or as in	sit or as in
	disháah	(I'm starting)	pique
o	doo	(not)	note

Vowels may be either long or short in duration, the long vowels being indicated by a doubling of the letter. This never affects the quality of the vowel, except that long i is always pronounced as in pique.

sis (belt) is short   siziiz (my belt) is long

Vowels with a hook beneath the letter are nasalized. That is, some of the breath passes through the nose in their production. After n, all vowels are nasalized and are not marked.

tsinaabąąs	(wagon)
jį́	(day)
kǫ́ǫ́	(here)

Diphthongs

The diphthongs are as follows:

ai	hai	(winter)	aisle
ei	séí	(sand)	weigh
oi	'ayóí	(very)	Joey

The diphthongs oi (as in Joey) will frequently be heard as ui (as in dewy) in certain sections of the reservation. However, since the related word ayóó is always of one value, this spelling has been standardized.

In a similar way, the diphtongs ei and ai are not universally distinguished. For example, the word for sand, séí will be pronounced sáí by some Navaho.

Consonants

The consonants are as follows:

b	bá	(for him)	like p in spot
d	díí	(this)	like t in stop
g	gah	(rabbit)	like k in sky

21

These sounds are not truly voiced as are the sounds represented by these letters in English, but are like the wholly unaspirated p, t, and k in the English words given as examples.

t	tó	(water)	tea
k	ké	(shoe)	kit

The t and k in Navaho are much more heavily aspirated than in English words given in the examples, so that the aspiration has a harsh fricative quality.

' glottal stop yá'át'ééh (it is good) unh unh, oh oh

In the American colloquial negative unh unh, or in the exclamatory expression oh oh, the glottal stop preceeds the u and the o respectively. Or, in actual speech, the difference between Johnny earns and Johnny yearns, is that the former has a glottal closure between the two words.

t'	yá'át'ééh	(it is good)

This letter represents the sound produced by the almost simultaneous release of the breath from the closure formed by the tip of the tongue and the teeth and the glottal closure described previously.

k'	k'ad	(now)

This sound is produced in the same way as the t', except that the k closure is formed by the back of the tongue and the soft palate.

m	mósí	(cat)	man
n	naadą́ą́'	(corn)	no
s	sis	(belt)	so
sh	shash	(bear)	she
z	zas	(snow)	zebra
zh	'ázhi'	(name)	azure
l	laanaa	(would that)	let
ł	łid	(smoke)	

This sound is made with the tongue in exactly the same position as in the ordinary l, but the voice box or larynx does not function. The difference between these two l's is the same as the difference between b and p, d and t, or s and z in English. If one attempts to pronounce th as in thin followed by l without an intervening vowel a ł is produced. Thus athłete.

h	háadi	(where)	hot

In Navaho there are two sounds represented by the letter h. The difference is in the intensity or fricativeness. Where h is the first letter in a syllable it is by some pronounce like the ch of German. This harsh pronunciation is the older, but the younger generation of Navaho tends to pronounce the sound much as in English.

gh	hooghan	(hogan)

This is the voiced equivalent of the harsh pronounced variety of h, the functioning of the voice being the only difference between the two sounds.

j   jádí   (antelope)   jug

This sound is an unaspirated ch, just as d and g represent unaspirated t and k.

ch   chizh   (wood)   church
ch'   ch'il   (plant)

This sound is produced in a fashion similar to the t' and k', but with the release of the breath from the ch position and from the glottal closure.

dz   dził   (mountain)   adze
ts   tsa   (awl)   hats

ts occurs in the beginning and middle of Navaho words, but only in final position English.

ts'   ts'in   (bone)

This sound is similar to ch', except for the tongue position, and involves the release of the breath from the glottal closure in the same way as the other glottalized sounds.

dl   beeldléí   (blanket)

The   dl   is   pronounced   as   one   sound   as   the   gl   is   in   the   word   glow.

tł   tła   (grease)

This sound is pronounced as unvoiced dl.

tł'   tł'ízí   (goat)

This sound involves the release of the breath from the t position of the tongue tip and teeth, from the contact of the sides of the tongue inside the back teeth (normal I position), and the glottal closure. It has a marked explosive quality. The sound is produced as a unit, as in the gl of glow, cited above.

y   yá   (sky)   you
w   'awéé'   (baby)   work

Palatalization and Labialization

It is to be noted that the sounds represented by g, t, k, h, gh, ch, and ts (when heavily aspirated are palatalized before e, i, and labialized before o. By this is meant that such a word as ké (shoe) is pronounced as though it were written kyé, and tó (water) as though written twó. Due to the nature of the gh sund, it practically resolves itself into a w when followed by o. Thus tálághosh (soap) could be written táláwosh, yishghoł (I'm running) as yishwoł etc. k and h can also be pronounced as kw and hw before e, i, in which case the combination is a distinct phoneme. In such cases the w must be written. Thus kwe'é (here), kwii (here), hwii (satisfaction) etc.

Tone

The present system of writing Navaho employs only one diacritical to express four tonal variations. This is the acute accent mark ('). If a short vowel or n, both elements of a long vowel, or a diphthong are marked thus the tone indicated is high. If only the first element of a long vowel or diphthong is marked the tone is falling from high, and if only the last element is marked the tone is rising from low. When a vowel, diphthong or n is unmarked the tone is low. The difference between low an high tone in Navaho is similar to a difference in tone of "are you" and "going" in the English question "are you going?"

'azee'	(medicine)	low tone
'azéé'	(mouth)	high tone

Word and Sentence Structure

Teachers will note that the possessive pronouns of Navaho are always prefixed to the noun. Thus, we have shimá (my mother), nimá (your mother), bimá (his mother), but never má. The stem –má has no independent form and never occurs without a prefix.

The structure of the Navaho verb has similar characteristics but is more complex. The subject of the sentence is always incorporated in the verb with a pronominal form, and other verbal elements. Ideas of time and mode are likewise incorporated in the verb, and auxiliary verbs such as will, did, have, might, etc. do not occur in Navaho. The ideas conveyed by these independent words in English are expressed by different forms of the verb itself in Navaho. Another point in which Navaho sentence structure differs from English is the English prepositions are postpositions in Navaho.

with my elder sister	shádí bił (my elder sister, with her)
for my mother	shimá bá (my mother for her)

Whereas normal word order in English is subject, verb, and object, Navaho has subject, object, and verb.